Dougie & V
The Story of a Flower and a Tree

by
Carly Jo Carson and Ben Sharony

Illustrated by
Nichole Graf

Dedicated to
Akiva, Cookie,
Frida, Henry,
Lua Bean
and Marbear.

Dougie was a Douglas Fir Tree...

and he was sick of it.

Being a tree sucks!
All we do is stand
here. Nothing happens.
I mean what's the
point anyway?

Man, look at that violet. She's so special.

Hey, you're
not so bad
yourself.

You're beautiful. I love the color of your petals. A purplish blue. So regal!

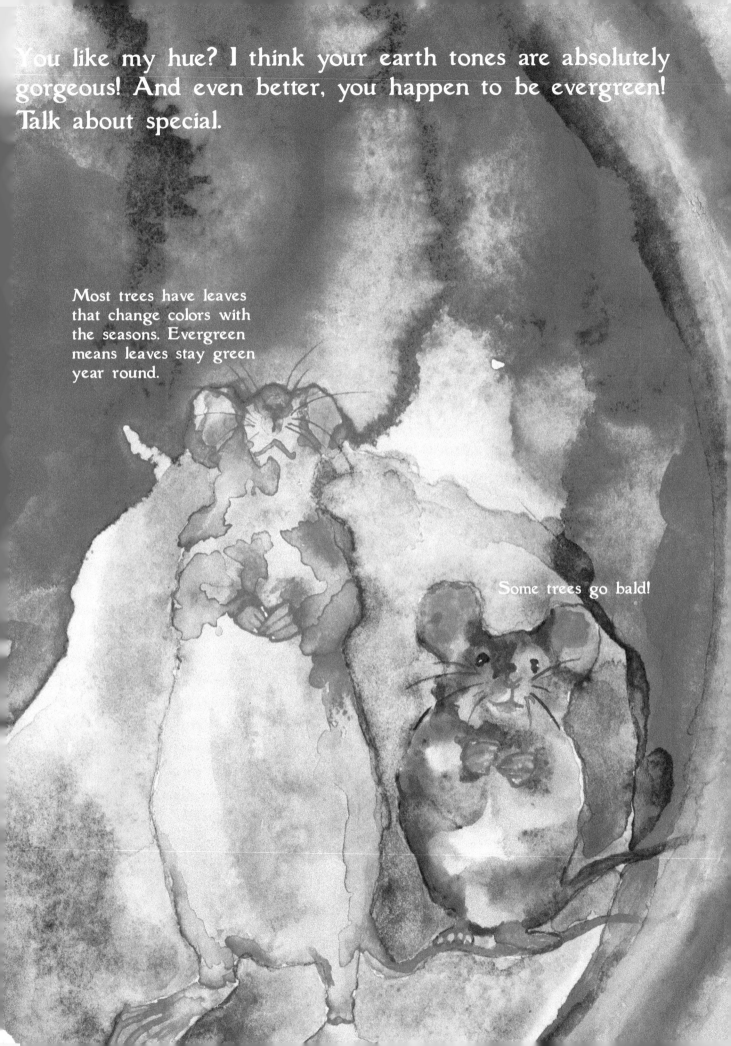

You like my hue? I think your earth tones are absolutely gorgeous! And even better, you happen to be evergreen! Talk about special.

Most trees have leaves that change colors with the seasons. Evergreen means leaves stay green year round.

Some trees go bald!

Special? Ya, right. I want to be more like you. Your fragrance is so...

INTOXICATING

Well, yeah, my smell is legendary. But it only lasts one sniff! I've never met anyone who doesn't savor the scent of a pine, spruce or fir tree. Your aroma is clean and crisp. Truly refreshing!

Violets are famous for their alluring scent. But it disappears after just one whiff.

Refreshing? Who cares! Anyway, it's so dark over here. Your home is amazing. So bright and sun-soaked.

D - As you grow up,
you'll get bigger and
move closer to the
s u n .

Sometimes you have to go through a

dark period before you can get to the light.

Doesn't matter.
I wish I was more like you, V.
So delicate and refined.

I'm not that strong.

But Dougie,
you're not seeing
how strong you are!

Not that strong? Are you completely PINE NUTS?!
Douglas firs have a husky, thick bark. It's SO strong, in
fact, it can protect you from fire!

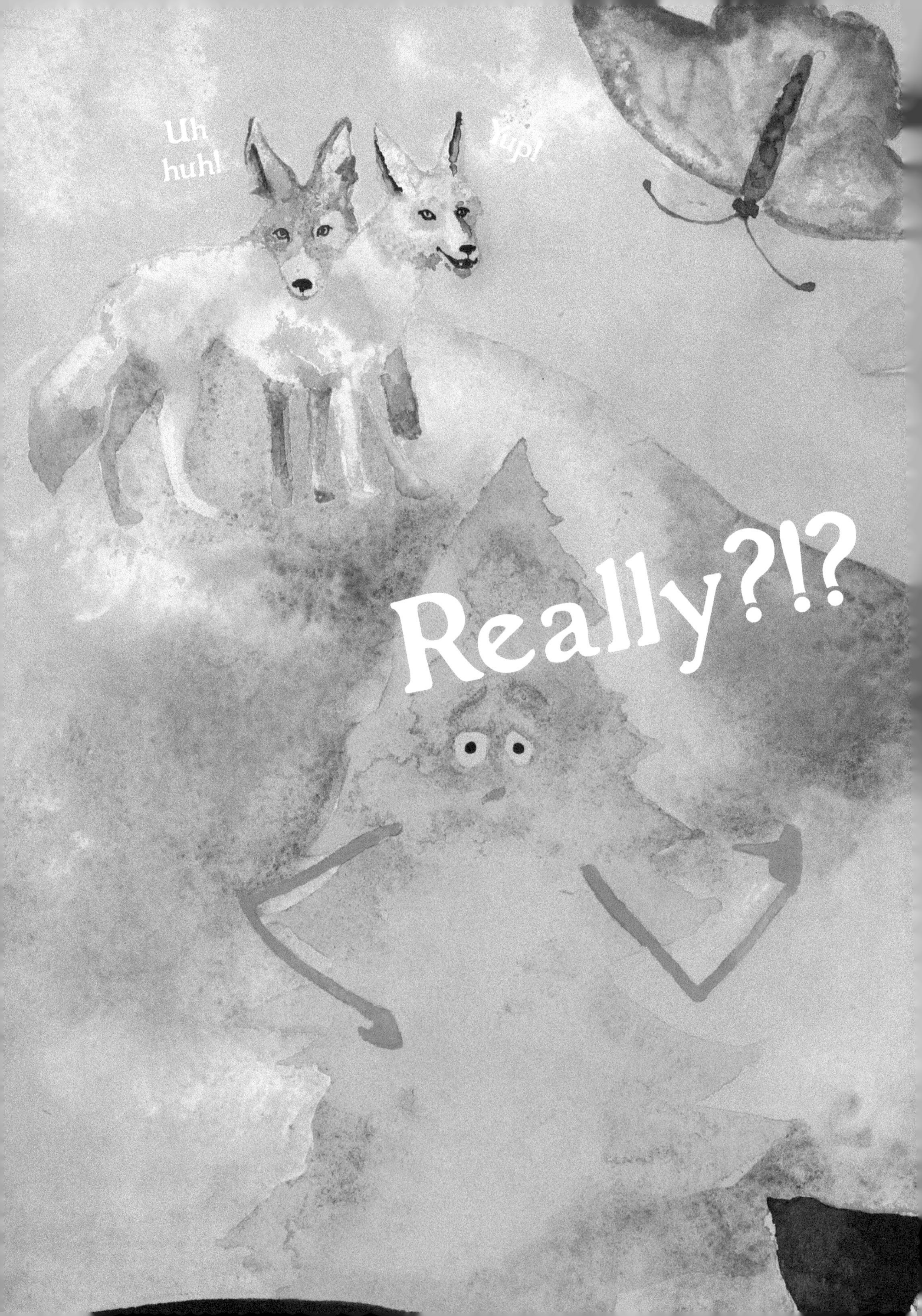
Uh
huh!
Yup!
Really?!?

And you might live to be 1000 years old!
Isn't that something?

I don't know. I guess that's okay.
But I wish I was popular like you.
The hummingbirds are obsessed
with you. And the bees just can't
get enough.

That's true. The hummingbirds
and I do have a good thing going.

Flowers and hummingbirds have what's known as a mutually beneficial relationship.

Some call it sssssymbiotic.

As we go from flower to flower sipping up nectar, we end up transferring pollen from one to the other. This is called "pollination." It's how flowers reproduce. But they're not the only ones. Insects, other birds, bats, and even cats also participate in the act of pollination.

Don't forget the wind!

eaters out there? We thought you should know that us hummingbirds eat more than our own weight in food everyday. Can you imagine eating your own weight in food?!

But Douglas you got it
too. Trees provide a home
to a number of birds and
small animals

Ya, but

And bears savor
your sap as a
special sweet treat.

Ya, but

And you provide sustenance (that means food) to a bunch of animals. Deer, mice, voles, birds, hares, brush rabbits, mountain beavers, pocket gophers, elk, and who am I forgetting?

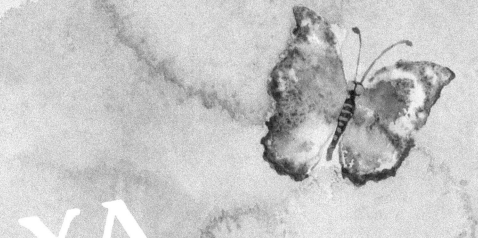

YA,

BUT

WHAT?!

Ya, but, well, I don't know! Even the humans love you. For them, you're a symbol of love and affection. You uplift their spirits. They couldn't care less about us.

Roughly half of the greenhouse effect is caused by CO_2. Therefore, trees are an essential part of our fight against global warming.

As they grow, trees absorb Carbon Dioxide (AKA CO_2) from the atmosphere and replace it with Oxygen (AKA O_2.)

On an emotional level,
you make them feel good.

Research shows, within minutes of being surrounded by trees, a person's blood pressure drops and their heart rate slows down, making them feel more calm and relaxed.

Kids love to play in and around you. Trees inspire adventure and spark imagination.

What adventures can
yooooouuuu
imagine?

People also love trees because, yes, they are beautiful.

And what's more, no two trees are alike. Which is a
good thing for you to remember, Dougie. Because

sometimes it's easier to see what's special about someone
else than it is to see what's special about yourself.

We all have strengths. And weaknesses.
What makes our world magical is that
we each have something unique to
give. We are all connected.
Look around you,
you will see!

Thank you
for showing
me, V!

You're welcome,
Douglas.

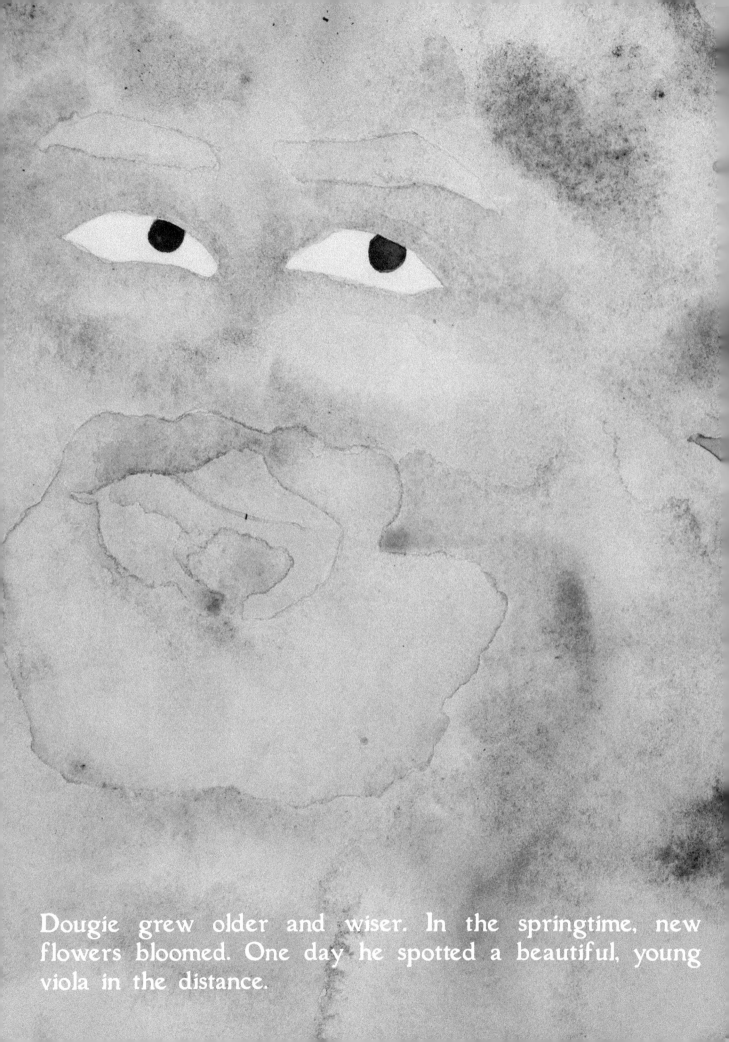

Dougie grew older and wiser. In the springtime, new flowers bloomed. One day he spotted a beautiful, young viola in the distance.

Man, everything stinks over here.
It's so hot and buggy!
Ah! Bugs all over!
They're really, really

BUGGING ME!

Wow, look at that beautiful
Douglas Fir tree. He seems
pretty special!

ABOUT THE AUTHORS

BEN SHARONY and **CARLY JO CARSON**
have been best friends since they were twelve. They are
passionate about sharing stories of transformation and
self-acceptance.

Ben is a filmmaker and an uncle and godfather.
bensharony.com

Carly is an artist, journey designer and mother of four.
carlyjocarson.com

ABOUT THE ILLUSTRATOR

NICHOLE GRAF
is a visual artist, nomad and sea witch.
ncgraf.com

Printed in the USA
CPSIA information can be obtained
at www.ICGtesting.com
LVHW071936110224
771576LV00023B/859